DEMOLITION EXPERTS

Ruth Owen and John Willis

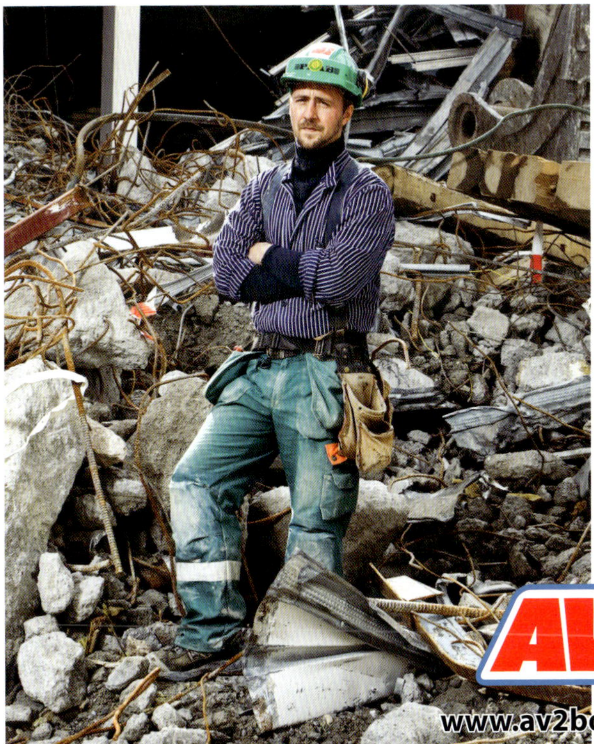

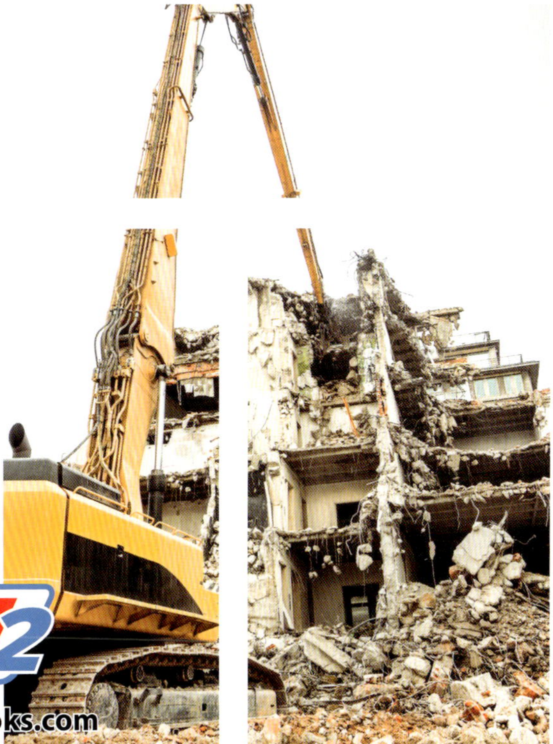

AV2

www.av2books.com

Step 1
Go to **www.av2books.com**

Step 2
Enter this unique code

KZLWEMRAG

Step 3
Explore your interactive eBook!

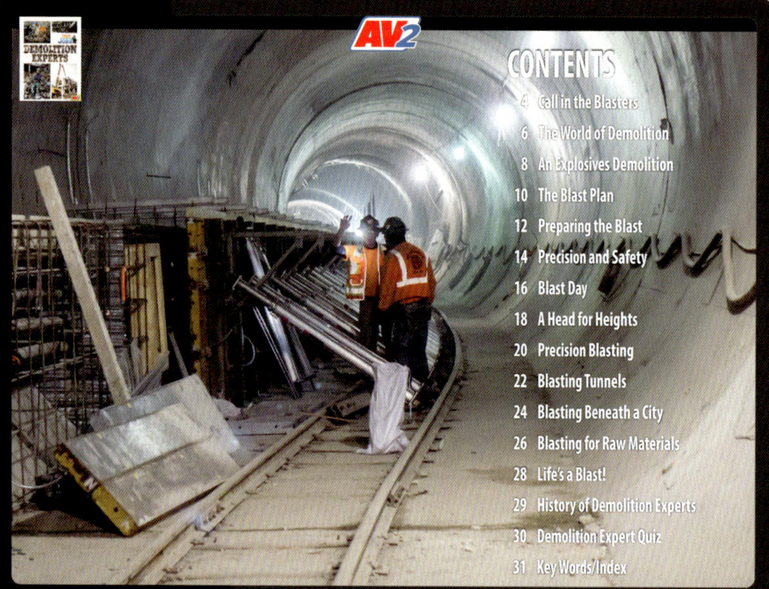

AV2 is optimized for use on any device

Your interactive eBook comes with...

Contents
Browse a live contents page to easily navigate through resources

Audio
Listen to sections of the book read aloud

Videos
Watch informative video clips

Weblinks
Gain additional information for research

Try This!
Complete activities and hands-on experiments

Key Words
Study vocabulary, and complete a matching word activity

Quizzes
Test your knowledge

Slideshows
View images and captions

... and much, much more!

DEMOLITION EXPERTS

Contents

Call in the Blasters

A hurricane-damaged 30-story building must be **demolished**. It is too difficult and dangerous to take apart the structure piece by piece. All around the **condemned** tower are shops, hotels, and people's homes that must not be harmed.

This is the challenge. So what is the solution? It is time to call in the demolition experts known as blasters.

Blasters are highly skilled **engineers** who rig a building with **dynamite**. The explosive **charges** are placed with absolute precision to ensure that a building collapses within a specific area. When the explosives are **detonated**, the building's framework must shatter. Then, **gravity** does the rest! It can take a team of blasters months to prepare a building for demolition. It takes less than 10 seconds for the building to be reduced to rubble!

The 1515 Tower in West Palm Beach, Florida, crumpled when 2,000 pounds (907 kilograms) of dynamite did its work.

After the demolition, all that was left of the 1515 Tower was a pile of gray rubble.

The first documented demolition was in **1773**. Holy Trinity Cathedral in Ireland was brought down by **150 pounds (68.04 kg)** of gunpowder.

The Royal Canberra Hospital in Australia was demolished. Debris shot as far as **1,640 feet (500 meters) away**. It killed one person and injured several others.

On **March 26, 2000**, the Seattle Kingdome set a **world record** for being the **largest** building ever demolished.

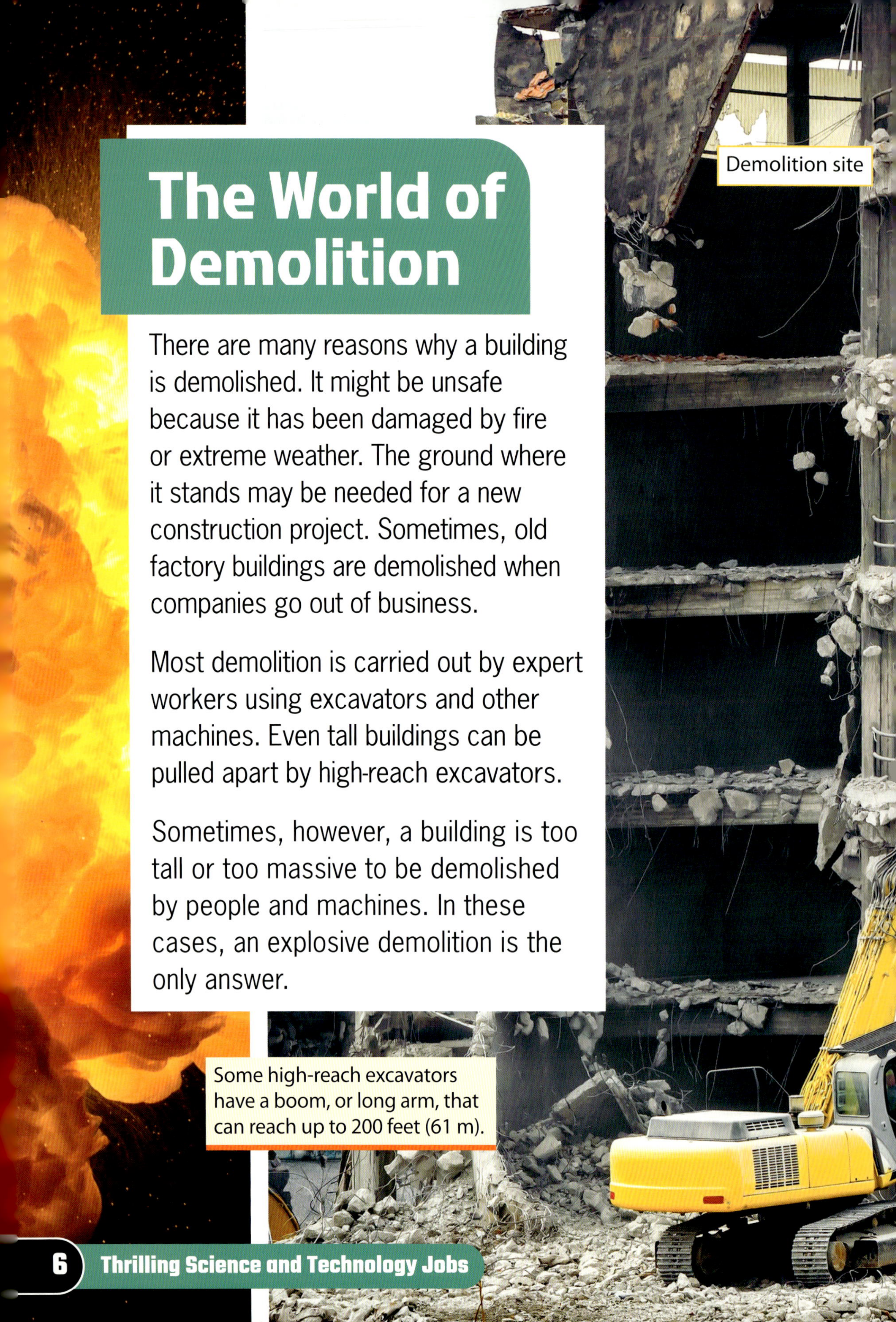

The World of Demolition

There are many reasons why a building is demolished. It might be unsafe because it has been damaged by fire or extreme weather. The ground where it stands may be needed for a new construction project. Sometimes, old factory buildings are demolished when companies go out of business.

Most demolition is carried out by expert workers using excavators and other machines. Even tall buildings can be pulled apart by high-reach excavators.

Sometimes, however, a building is too tall or too massive to be demolished by people and machines. In these cases, an explosive demolition is the only answer.

Some high-reach excavators have a boom, or long arm, that can reach up to 200 feet (61 m).

Jaw-like tools are attached to an excavator's boom. These powerful tools can tear down walls, crush concrete, and cut through steel.

EXPLOSIVE

Demolition experts try to recycle metal, bricks, and other materials. Excavators scoop chunks of concrete and other debris into a rubble crusher. This material is crushed and can be used as part of the **foundation** for a new building.

An Explosives Demolition

When blasters demolish a building, they place just the right amount of explosives in exactly the right places to destroy parts of the building's structure. Once its structure is weakened, a building's weight and gravity bring it down.

Explosives engineers control which way a building falls by placing explosives in specific parts of the building. Then, they detonate them in the right order. If a building needs to topple toward the north into an unused parking lot, they detonate explosives on the north side of the building first. Then, the building's north side topples and pulls the rest of the building with it.

A building may be surrounded on all four sides by streets, homes, and other structures. In this case, a difficult and risky operation called an **implosion** is carried out. The explosives are set up so that the building collapses straight down into its own **footprint**.

The Central Police Station in Christchurch, New Zealand, was expertly brought down in May 2015. The building had been damaged by an earthquake.

Tallest Demolitions

Scale 250 miles
0 402 kilometers

Landmark Tower, Fort Worth, Texas
After a tornado damaged the Landmark Tower in 2000, the 380-foot (116-m) building was demolished.

Ocean Tower, South Padre Island, Texas
The Ocean Tower never opened. Cracks were found in its support columns. In 2009, the 379-foot (115-m) building came down.

J. L. Hudson's Department Store and Addition, Detroit, Michigan
The 439-foot (134-m) building was demolished in 1998. At the time, it was the tallest building ever to be imploded.

The Blast Plan

Once a team of blasters is hired to demolish a building, they must carefully plan the project. They begin by examining old **blueprints** of the building. These highly detailed plans show a building's structure and what it is made of.

The team visits the derelict building to assess its construction. How deep are the concrete columns that hold up each story? Could there be thick steel beams inside the columns?

Blasters may spend weeks in a dusty, dangerous old building making detailed notes. With no elevators in operation, this can mean climbing up and down cold, dark stairwells hundreds of times!

Once all the **data** is collected, the team designs a blast plan.

Blueprints are drawn by a building's designer, or architect. They show construction workers exactly how to put together the building.

Life as a blaster means wearing protective clothing, such as a hard hat, steel-capped boots, or fluorescent overalls.

EXPLOSIVE

An explosives engineer might use a computer program to create a 3D model of the building. Then, the explosives are added to the model and the engineer runs a virtual test of the blast to see how the building will collapse.

Preparing the Blast

With a blast plan in place, the blasters get to work drilling thousands of holes in the sections of the building that will be blown up. Each hole is then packed with an explosive charge.

To blow up concrete, blasters usually use dynamite. To demolish parts of a building made of steel, an explosive called cyclotrimethylenetrinitramine is used. This explosive is also known as RDX or Research Development Formula. When is ignited, it expands at 5 miles per second (8 kilometers per second), slicing through thick steel.

To ignite a charge, it must be connected to a **detonator** outside the building. This is done with a long cord called a detonating cord or det-cord. The blasters lay miles of det-cord throughout the building, connecting all the explosive charges to the detonator.

Setting up the thousands of explosive charges inside a building may take a team of blasters several weeks or even months.

Workers may cut through steel supports on bridges that are being prepared for blasting.

An Explosive Charge

A traditional det-cord contains material that burns steadily. When the det-cord is lit, the flame travels along the cord and ignites the blasting cap.

Today, det-cords usually carry an electrical charge that ignites the blasting cap.

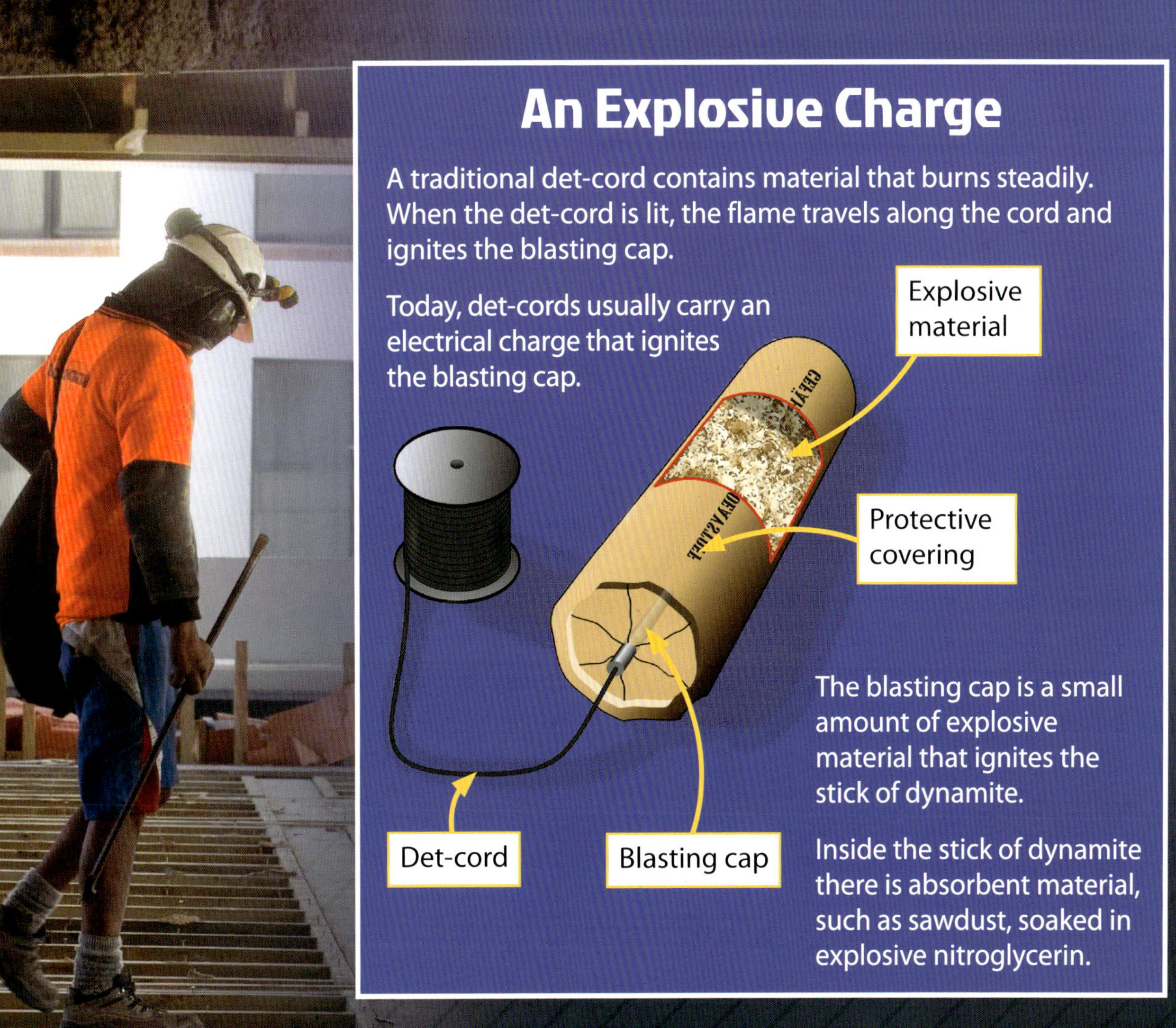

The blasting cap is a small amount of explosive material that ignites the stick of dynamite.

Inside the stick of dynamite there is absorbent material, such as sawdust, soaked in explosive nitroglycerin.

Demolition workers in Christchurch, New Zealand, prepared buildings such as the Grand Chancellor Hotel for demolition following an earthquake in 2011.

EXPLOSIVE

Before the blasters start work, a destruction crew might weaken a structure so it gives way more easily. The crew removes inside walls and fractures concrete columns by smashing them with sledgehammers.

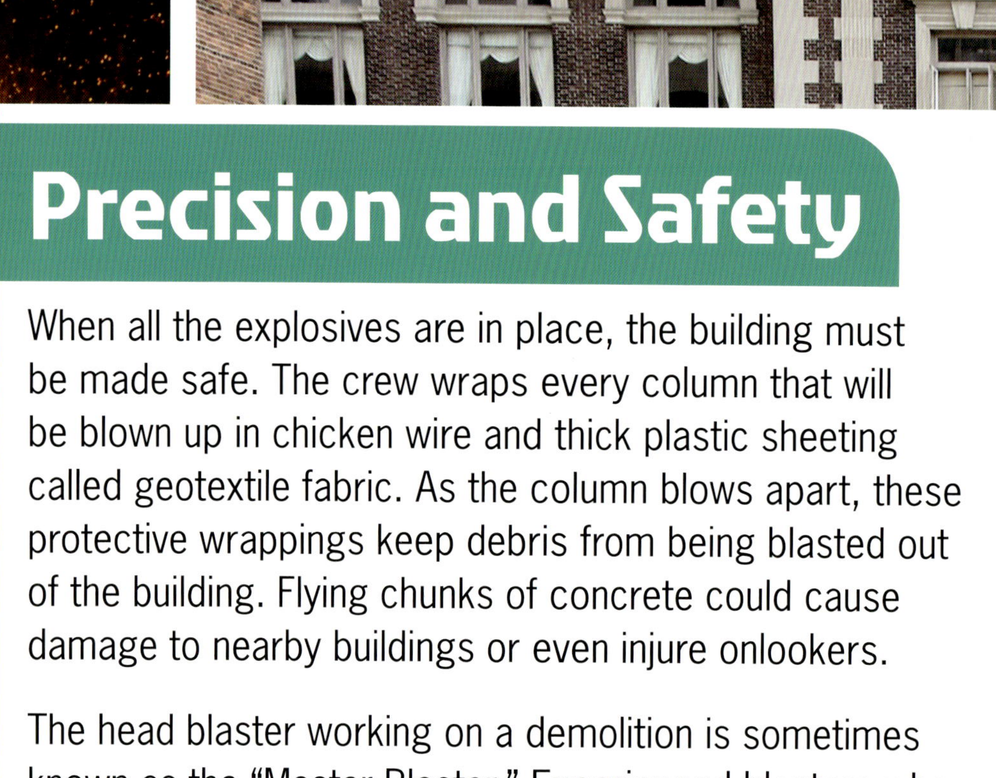

Precision and Safety

When all the explosives are in place, the building must be made safe. The crew wraps every column that will be blown up in chicken wire and thick plastic sheeting called geotextile fabric. As the column blows apart, these protective wrappings keep debris from being blasted out of the building. Flying chunks of concrete could cause damage to nearby buildings or even injure onlookers.

The head blaster working on a demolition is sometimes known as the "Master Blaster." Experienced blasters who have demolished lots of buildings may also be given this title. The blasters' work must be absolutely precise. Every detail is checked again and again. If the explosives are placed incorrectly, the building might fall in the wrong direction, crushing neighboring buildings. If a mistake is made, the building might only partially fall. Then, the explosives crew would be left with an unstable, potentially lethal structure that could collapse at any time.

Geotextile fabric

Geotextile fabric is often wrapped around the outside of a condemned building. This ensures that debris does not fly around and helps protect the environment.

In 2013, a building collapsed in Philadelphia during a nearby demolition. A total of 6 people were killed, while 14 were injured.

EXPLOSIVE

Before the big day, an exclusion zone is set up around the blast site. Security guards might be hired to patrol the area. This ensures that no one, except the blasting crew, can get close to the building.

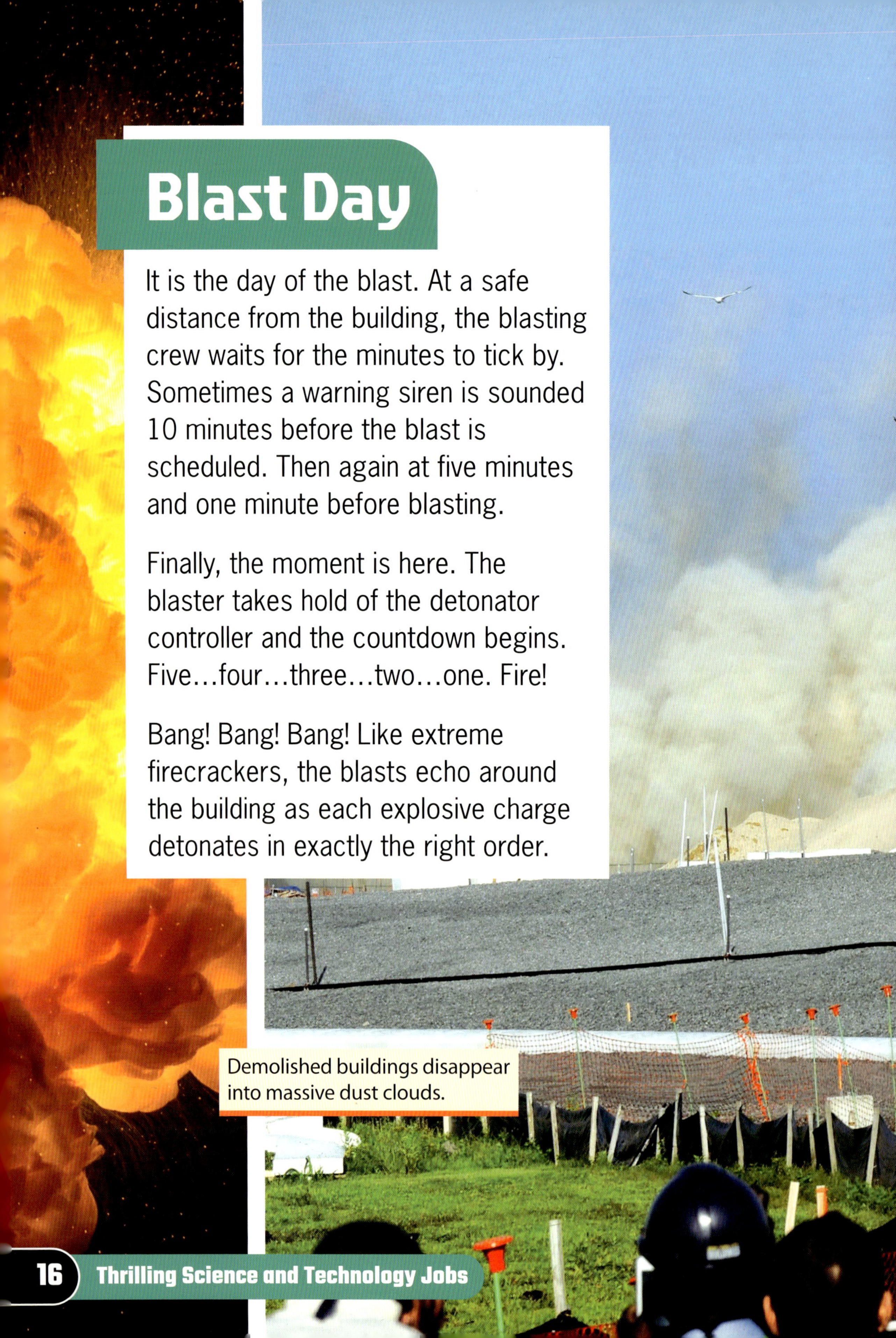

Blast Day

It is the day of the blast. At a safe distance from the building, the blasting crew waits for the minutes to tick by. Sometimes a warning siren is sounded 10 minutes before the blast is scheduled. Then again at five minutes and one minute before blasting.

Finally, the moment is here. The blaster takes hold of the detonator controller and the countdown begins. Five…four…three…two…one. Fire!

Bang! Bang! Bang! Like extreme firecrackers, the blasts echo around the building as each explosive charge detonates in exactly the right order.

Demolished buildings disappear into massive dust clouds.

Radios must be kept away from detonators when they are in use.

EXPLOSIVE

A crew watches videos of a blast and carefully examines the site to make sure that every charge exploded. Any charges that did not detonate must be found and removed.

A Head for Heights

Some jobs require a blaster to have a head for extreme heights!

For decades, many power plants have generated electricity by burning coal. Today, some of these environmentally unfriendly coal-fired power plants are being decommissioned or shut down. When this happens, the blasters may be called in to demolish the power plant's giant **cooling tower**, high chimney stack, and other structures.

To ensure that the tower crumples in on itself, the blasting crew drills thousands of holes at precise locations high up the tower and at its base. Then, the holes are packed with explosives. The crew needs to ensure that the tower does not fall toward the highway that runs alongside it.

Other kinds of power plants have cooling towers, too. In 2006, the Trojan Cooling Tower was the first large nuclear plant in the United States to be decommissioned and demolished.

Almost 2,800 pounds (1224.69 kg) of dynamite was used to demolish the Trojan Cooling Tower.

EXPLOSIVE

In order to set up explosives, blasters may work inside a cooling tower. They may also work from a cradle dangling on the outside of a tower.

Precision Blasting

On September 26, 2015, two years of detailed planning and hard work came to an end with the dramatic demolition of Cockenzie Power Station's twin chimney stacks. The coal-fired power plant in Scotland had been in operation for 45 years. Now the plant was closed. The land would be **redeveloped**.

At 489 feet (149 m) high, each of the chimneys was taller than a 40-story building. A blast plan was devised to make the chimneys fall toward each other and impact 459 feet (140 m) above the ground. To achieve this, the blasting team drilled 1,500 holes in each chimney and packed them with explosives. The blasters' plan went without a hitch, and the chimneys crashed to the ground in a cloud of dust and rubble!

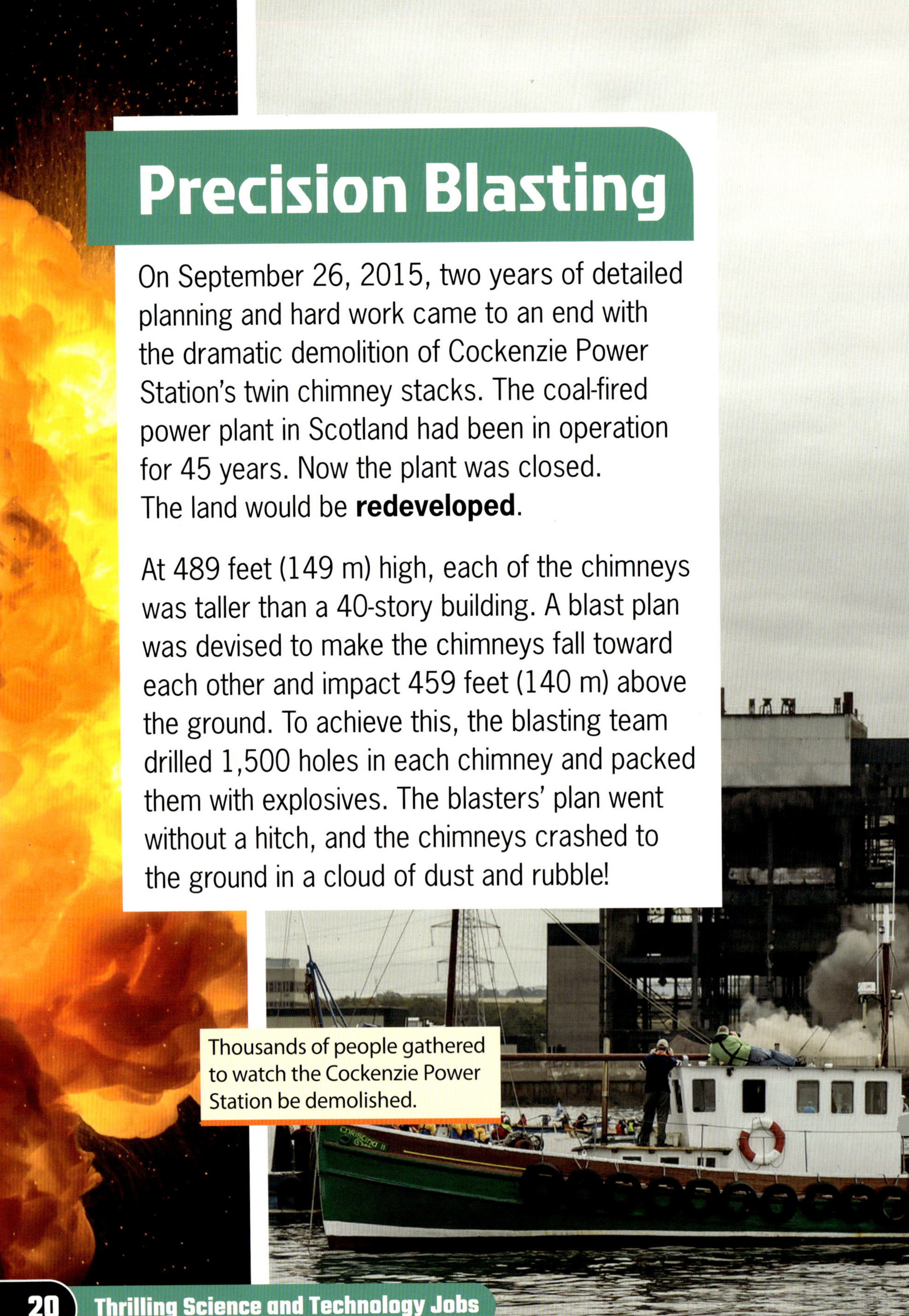

Thousands of people gathered to watch the Cockenzie Power Station be demolished.

Cockenzie's turbine hall, where the electricity was once generated, was sent crashing to the ground just after the chimneys.

EXPLOSIVE

When Cockenzie Power Station was blasted, a local resident, Donald McCulloch, won a raffle. He became a blaster for the day and got to push the "fire" button!

Blasting Tunnels

If you have ever ridden on a subway or traveled through a mountain tunnel, you probably have explosives engineers to thank for your journey. Some explosives engineers use their skills to work on challenging tunneling projects, often deep underground.

To blast a tunnel through solid rock, engineers use a process called the "drill and blast" method. A machine called a drilling jumbo is used to drill a pattern of holes in the rock face. Then, the holes are filled with explosives.

When the explosives are detonated, the rock face cracks, breaking up into rubble that can be hauled away.

Just as in demolition blasting, the placing of the explosives to blast a tunnel must be highly accurate. Get the blast wrong, and it could start a rock slide above ground or cause the tunnel to collapse. If the team is tunneling under a city, a mistake could damage buildings or roads on the surface.

On a tunneling project, an explosives engineer will work with rock scientists called geologists. A geologist gathers data on the rock's hardness and how its layers have formed. This data is used to create the blasting plan.

The angle, size, and spacing of the holes used in "drill and blast" methods must suit the make-up of the rock being blasted.

The **Malpas-Tunnel** in France was **the first tunnel** built through the help of explosives. It was built between **1679 and 1681**.

During the **mid-1800s**, explosives were used to build **19 tunnels** along the **Transcontinental Railway** in the United States.

The **Gotthard Railway Tunnel** in Switzerland was opened in **1882**. At the time, it was the **longest tunnel** constructed by dynamite.

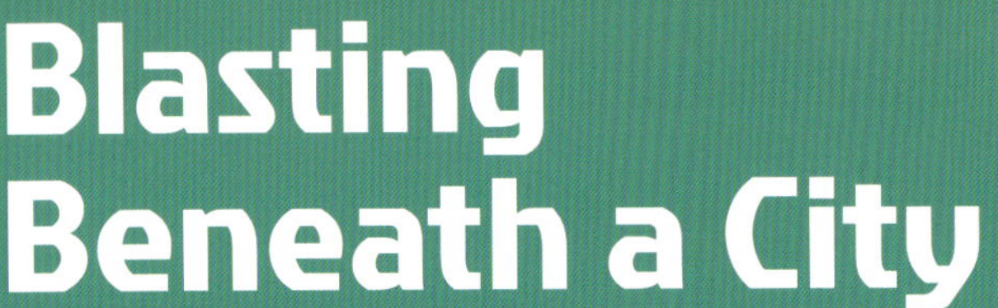

Blasting Beneath a City

Deep below the bustling streets of New York City, explosives engineers are hard at work in a subterranean world. These engineers are working on the East Side Access project. They are building train tunnels, platform areas where people will catch trains, and shafts for elevators and escalators.

Each day, the blasters descend more than 10 stories beneath the city streets. Here, water drips from the rocky ceilings of the tunnels and enormous caverns. The dusty air is filled with the hum of heavy machinery.

Using the drill and blast method, these engineers are blasting through rock that is more than 350 million years old. One day in the future, more than 160,000 people will travel through these tunnels every day.

The East Side Access project is planned to open in December 2022.

The explosive engineers and other workers who build tunnels beneath New York City are known as Sandhogs.

EXPLOSIVE

Some of the tunneling for the East Side Access project has been carried out by blasting. A giant tunnel-boring machine has also been used.

Blasting for Raw Materials

Some explosives experts work in mines. They blast rock to reach coal or obtain ores, which are rocks that contain metal. Others work in quarries, blasting rock from the ground to be used in construction.

A blast engineer at a quarry might need to design a blast plan that fragments a rock face, turning it into a giant heap of rubble. This broken rock is used as a base material beneath sidewalks, roads, and buildings. Crushed rock is also mixed with sand, cement, and water to make concrete.

An explosives engineer at a quarry might have to blast a house-sized, 40,000-pound (18,144-kg) block of granite from a rock face. Cutting machines are then used to cut the rock into smaller blocks. The granite might be used as blocks for building houses, pavement, or kitchen countertops.

Cutting rocks such as granite into blocks makes it easier to store and move them.

To break a rock face into rubble, a blast engineer digs holes into it. They are filled with explosives. The explosives are detonated, shattering the rock.

EXPLOSIVE

Houses, apartment buildings, sidewalks, roads, school buildings, cars, planes, computers, coins, even soda cans...without the work of explosives engineers in mines and quarries, we would not have the raw materials to make all these things.

Life's a Blast!

A blasting project involves day after day of painstaking preparation work. Then, finally, the big day arrives. The tension is almost unbearable as the explosives detonate. A blaster knows instantly if she or he has gotten it right, or if something has gone wrong.

Boom! If all that is left is an enormous heap of debris, the blaster can feel relief and pride at a job well done. If something has not gone according to plan, the blaster must carefully assess what went wrong, and then use this information when planning future blasts.

Explosive demolition is an unusual and potentially dangerous career. But if you like the idea of combining detailed, meticulous engineering and science work with the high drama of explosions, blasting could just be the life for you!

If rules, laws, and safety regulations are followed, explosive demolition can be a fun career.

History of Demolition Experts

Explosives have been used in demolition since the 1600s. Over the years, these demolitions have become safer and more controlled.

1627 Gunpowder is used in mining for the first time in Banska Stiavnica, a Slovakian town.

1679 The Malpas-Tunnel in France is the first-ever tunnel constructed using explosives.

1773 Holy Trinity Cathedral is the first building demolished by explosives.

1867 Dynamite is invented and patented, creating safer and more powerful explosions.

1990 4.63 billion pounds (2.1 billion kg) of explosives are used for mining in the United States.

1994 The demolition of the Sears Merchandise Center in Philadelphia draws a crowd of 50,000 spectators.

2007 Construction begins on the East Side Access Tunnel in New York City.

2019 Martin Tower, a 331.4-foot (101-m) building in Pennsylvania, is brought down in a matter of seconds. It will take up to a year to clear debris from the grounds.

Demolition Expert Quiz

01 When was dynamite created?

02 What is a head blaster called?

03 Where does a demolition engineer blast granite?

04 How are subway tunnels made?

05 Which tall Detroit building was imploded in 1998?

06 What is wrapped around a building to keep spectators safe?

07 Which long tunnel was made using dynamite and opened in 1882?

08 How many people will travel in the East Side Access Tunnel per day upon its completion?

09 What is the full name of the explosive used to demolish steel?

10 Which 30-story Florida building needed to be demolished because of hurricane damage?

ANSWER

01 1867 **02** Master blaster **03** In a quarry **04** By using drills and explosives underground **05** J. L. Hudson's Department Store **06** Geotextile fabric **07** Gotthard Railway Tunnel **08** More than 160,000 **09** Cyclotrimethylenetrinitramine **10** 1515 Tower

Key Words

blueprints: detailed technical drawings that show the design of a building, vehicle, or machine

charges: explosives, such as inside a stick of dynamite, that are connected to a detonating cord

condemned: in the case of a building, judged unfit or unsafe to be used

cooling tower: a large chimney-like tower that is used to remove heat from a power plant or other type of factory

data: information and facts, often in the form of numbers

demolished: taken apart or destroyed

detonated: caused something to explode

detonator: a control device connected to an explosive charge by a detonating cord; when fired, the detonator causes the charge to explode

dynamite: a type of explosive made of absorbent material soaked in nitroglycerin; it is usually in the form of a stick or tube

engineers: people who use math, science, and technology to design, build, repair, or demolish machines or structures

footprint: the amount of space on the ground that is covered by a building or other structure

foundation: the part of a building or other structure that connects it to the ground

gravity: the force that causes objects to be pulled toward other objects

implosion: a controlled blast that causes a building or other structure to collapse within its own footprint

redeveloped: used for new construction projects

Index

Get the best of both worlds.

AV2 bridges the gap between print and digital.

The expandable resources toolbar enables quick access to content including **videos**, **audio**, **activities**, **weblinks**, **slideshows**, **quizzes**, and **key words**.

Animated videos make static images come alive.

Resource icons on each page help readers to further **explore key concepts**.

Published by AV2
350 5th Avenue, 59th Floor
New York, NY 10118
Website: www.av2books.com

Library of Congress Control Number: 2019957548

ISBN 978-1-7911-2201-0 (hardcover)
ISBN 978-1-7911-2199-0 (softcover)
ISBN 978-1-7911-2200-3 (multi-user eBook)
ISBN 978-1-7911-2202-7 (single-user eBook)

Printed in Guangzhou, China
1 2 3 4 5 6 7 8 9 0 24 23 22 21 20

032020
101319

Project Coordinator: John Willis
Designer: Terry Paulhus

Every reasonable effort has been made to trace ownership and to obtain permission to reprint copyright material. The publishers would be pleased to have any errors or omissions brought to their attention so that they may be corrected in subsequent printings.

AV2 acknowledges Alamy, Getty Images, Newscom, Shutterstock, and Wikimedia as its primary image suppliers for this title.

First published in 2017 by Ruby Tuesday Books Ltd.